Located in Paducah, Kentucky, the American Quilter's Society (AQS) is dedicated to promoting the accomplishments of today's quilters. Through its publications and events, AQS strives to honor today's quiltmakers and their work and to inspire future creativity and innovation in quiltmaking.

EXECUTIVE BOOK EDITOR: ELAINE H. BRELSFORD
BOOK EDITOR: LINDA BAXTER LASCO
COPY EDITOR: CHRYSTAL ABHALTER
PROOFREADER: JOANN TREECE
GRAPHIC DESIGN: SARAH BOZONE
COVER DESIGN: MICHAEL BUCKINGHAM
QUILT PHOTOGRAPHY: CHARLES R. LYNCH

All rights reserved. No part of this book may be reproduced, stored in any retrieval system, or transmitted in any form, or by any means including but not limited to electronic, mechanical, photocopy, recording or otherwise, without the written consent of the author and publisher. Patterns may be copied for personal use only, including the right to enter contests; quilter should seek written permission from the author and pattern designer before entering. Credit must be given to the author, pattern designer, and publisher on the quilt label and contest entry form. Written permission from author, pattern designer, and publisher must be sought to raffle or auction quilts made from this book. While every effort has been made to ensure that the contents of this publication are as accurate and correct as possible, no warranty is provided nor results guaranteed. Since the author and AQS have no control over individual skills or choice of materials and tools, they do not assume responsibility for the use of this information.

Additional copies of this book may be ordered from the American Quilter's Society, PO Box 3290, Paducah, KY 42002-3290, or online at www.AmericanQuilter.com.

Text © 2014, Author, Kent Mick
Artwork © 2014, American Quilter's Society

American Quilter's Society

PO Box 3290 • Paducah, KY 42002-3290
Fax 270-898-1173 • email: orders@AQSquilt.com

Library of Congress Cataloging-in-Publication Data

Mick, Kent.
 Free-motion quilting on your home sewing machine / by Kent Mick.
    pages cm
Includes bibliographical references and index.
ISBN 978-1-60460-151-0 (alk. paper)
1. Machine quilting. I. Title.
TT835.M5124 2014
746.46--dc23

Contents

Meet the Author Kent Mick

In 2003, Kent made doll beds for two of his granddaughters for Christmas. His wife, Judy, suggested they make quilts for them.

Neither had ever quilted before but they worked together to make miniature quilts for the beds. Kent fell in love with the process. That started his quilting career, which has continued unabated since his retirement in 2009 after 40 years as an auto mechanic.

Other than his love of quilting and helping people learn to quilt and improve their quilting skills, there are many other areas of his life he enjoys—most particularly his wife, two children, and eight grandchildren.

He is an avid swimmer, a swimming instructor, a lifeguard, ...d enjoys scuba diving. Woodworking, as evidenced by ...e doll beds, is another hobby he pursues.

...ent and Judy enjoy traveling together. For the past several ...ears, Kent has been involved in tracing the genealogy of ...neir families.

Introduction

I have been helping people learn how to quilt on their home sewing machines since 2006. In that time, many of the people have recommended that I write a book about machine quilting, so here it is.

Free-motion quilting is relatively easy to do but does require practice. I will give you a step-by-step process to follow to learn how to quilt your quilts. The idea is to show you the basic techniques of free-motion quilting, not to present every design that is available. Once you learn the basics, you will be able to do any design you want.

There are two main reasons to do your own quilting.

 First, you can save a lot of money doing it yourself rather than paying to have it done.

 **Second,** for me, I like to do the entire quilt myself. If I have a quilt quilted by someone else, it would then belong to me AND whoever did the quilting. I guess I am selfish that way.

I like to stress that this is the way I do my quilting. There are several ways of doing many of these techniques, so if you have been doing something in a certain way and like it better than my way, by all means continue with yours.

I have included practice exercises and how to quilt by zones.

I recommend reading through everything first to familiarize yourself with the process, then to reread it and do the practice exercises as you go along.

Do not get discouraged, as it will take practice to achieve the desired results. If you have a problem with a certain exercise, do it again until you have it down fairly well. You will probably not feel very proficient until you have done several practice pieces, but stick with it. You will improve. You don't have to be artistic to machine quilt.

Quilting your own quilts on your home machine saves you both the expense and space a longarm would take up. So sit back, relax, have fun, and learn to quilt your quilts.

Supplies

Sewing machine. It doesn't need a big throat. A regular machine will do. You'll need to drop the feed dogs. If your feed dogs don't drop, you can cover them with a business card.

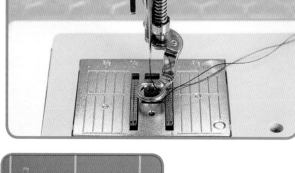

Free-motion foot. Some manufacturers call this a darning foot or embroidery foot. It is spring-loaded so that it is capable of floating over the quilt as you sew. Some are plastic and some are metal. They have a round or oval foot. Some are open in front and some are closed. If you have a closed foot, I recommend cutting the front open to have a better view of your quilt stitches.

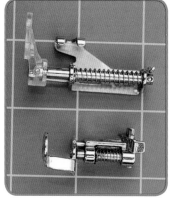

Thread. I recommend cotton—both dark and light.

Water-soluble thread

Paper and pencil

Approximately a dozen 12" x 12" squares of plain white or cream-colored fabric and six 12" x 12" squares of darker fabric. Inexpensive muslin or scrap fabric will do. Nine 12" x 12" and two 14" x 14" squares of batting.

White pounce pad. I recommend the iron-out powder pad.

A blue or red pounce pad. More on these later (page 26).

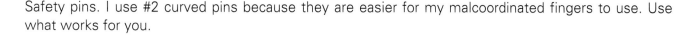

Water-soluble marking pens

Rotary cutter, mat, and ruler

Safety pins. I use #2 curved pins because they are easier for my malcoordinated fingers to use. Use what works for you.

Quilting gloves. I like to use these and highly recommend them. If I am quilting small areas, I will only wear the right glove, leaving my left hand free to cut thread, etc.

Basic sewing supplies: scissors, seam ripper (which I refer to as my de-sewer), and so on. (Yes, you will make mistakes that you will want to take out, but don't remove any mistakes from your practice pieces. Just keep moving.)

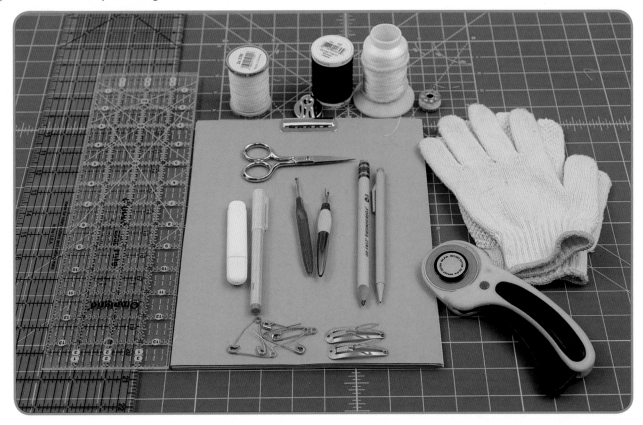

Glad® Press'n Seal. This can be found in the grocery store in the plastic wrap and foil section.

I recommend using a Teflon® sheet on the bed of your sewing machine. It will make the fabric slide with much less effort. I use the Supreme Slider (www.freemotionslider.com).

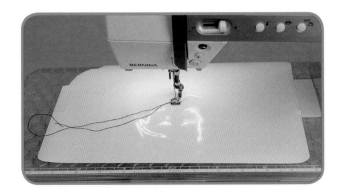

How to Quilt

Regulating the Stitch Length

When you sew with your sewing machine, the stitch length setting determines the length of the stitches. The stitch length is accomplished by the feed dogs moving the fabric at the stitch setting on your machine. For example, if you have your machine set to make 10 stitches to the inch, every time the needle goes down and up the feed dog will move the fabric 1/10 of an inch and in one inch you will get 10 stitches.

In free-motion quilting you drop the feed dogs down so they don't touch the fabric. Therefore, YOU determine the stitch length by how quickly the needle goes up and down combined with how quickly you move the fabric under the needle.

If your needle speed is too fast or you move the fabric too slowly, you will get too many stitches per inch. If the needle speed is too slow or you move the fabric too quickly, you will get too few stitches per inch. The main thing is to try to be consistent with your stitch length. I have found that it is better to have too many stitches per inch than to have too few. It just looks better.

You will practice stitch length in Exercise 1 (page 6).

Positioning Your Hands

Pretend that your hands are a small quilt frame. You will do your quilting within this space. If you start to sew too close to your hands, stop sewing, reposition your hands, and start again.

If your machine has the needle down option, set it so that when you stop the needle is down, holding your work in place. Then you are in the right place to start sewing again after you reposition your hands.

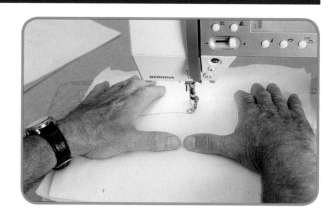

Make sure the needle is straight before you start sewing. It can be pulled and bent by the fabric, causing a jagged stitch when you start sewing.

Now, one of the most important things to remember about free-motion quilting is to NEVER TURN YOUR FABRIC! You will learn to quilt by moving your fabric in different directions without turning it. I realize that with a small piece (like our 12" practice pieces), it is tempting to turn the fabric in different directions. But if you are quilting a large quilt on your

machine, each time you change directions you would have to stuff the whole quilt through the throat of your machine, which is time consuming and awkward.

Imagine stitching in the ditch (exactly on the edge of the pattern pieces) along the sides of a 6" eight-pointed star. You would sew along one point, stop at the tip, turn the quilt in the machine, sew down to the next point, turn again to sew to the tip, and so on. You would have to turn the quilt 16 times to quilt one star!

Practicing Free-Motion Quilting

Exercise 1: Practice stitch length on paper.

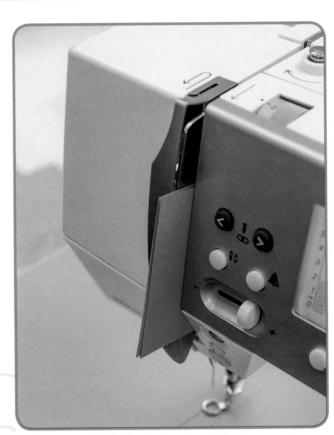

In this exercise you will learn to get into a rhythm of sewing a consistent stitch length by practicing sewing on a piece of paper with no thread in your machine.

Remove the thread and bobbin from your machine.

Note that some sewing machines will not sew without thread in them. Consult your owner's manual to see if you can override this feature. On some machines, you can insert a card into the thread path to fool it into thinking it has thread.

Overriding the "no thread" feature

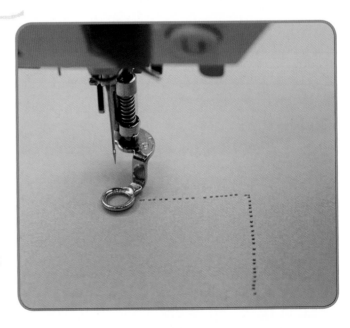

With your hands properly placed on the paper, start your needle moving slowly by pressing lightly on the foot control. Start moving your paper straight up and then move to the right. Move down, to the left, up, and around—all without turning the paper.

Continue moving in this manner—up and down and back and forth—until you achieve fairly consistent stitch length; that is, the holes made by the needle are evenly spaced. Start out slowly. Increase your speed but stay within your comfort level. Speed will come with practice.

Remember, if your hands get too close to the needle, STOP. Reposition your hands and start again. This will help you maintain your stitch length and alignment.

Make circles by moving the paper in a circular manner.

Write your name or make a flower— whatever comes to mind.

Take your paper out. Hold it up and look at the holes. Are they fairly evenly spaced? Note that they will not be perfect. This is all right. You will get better with practice.

If your holes are too far apart you need to EITHER increase the speed the needle moves up and down OR slow down how quickly you move the paper under the needle. If your holes are too close together, you need to EITHER slow down the needle OR speed up how you move the paper. If your holes in the paper are not as they should be, practice some more until they look fairly evenly spaced.

Holes too far apart

Holes too close together

When you sew curves, keep the speed of the needle fast enough so that the curves appear rounded and not as a series of straight lines.

Exercise 2: Pull up your bobbin thread.

In this exercise you will learn the why and how of pulling your bobbin thread to the top of your quilt.

If you don't pull your bobbin thread to the top of your quilt when you start to sew, you run the risk of catching it under your quilt and causing a bird's nest (a huge blob of thread) on the underside of the quilt.

On a personal note, I have never understood how the needle can go up and down two times and leave what seems like 100 yards of thread packed up under your quilt! Oh well.

Pulling the bobbin thread up when you are done eliminates having to cut all the threads on the underside of the quilt. When you finish sewing one area, you can pull the bobbin thread to the top and clip it before moving on to the next area. You don't have to lift your quilt up and use scissors to cut the bottom thread, saving time and eliminating the possibility of accidently clipping your quilt backing.

Practice this technique every time you are free-motion quilting. After you have done it several times it will become natural and you will do it without even thinking about it.

Follow these instructions step by step as you do each step on the sewing machine. It may take several times of practicing it before you can finally do it without rereading the "When Starting to Sew" section. Use a contrasting thread so you can see your stitches.

WHEN STARTING TO SEW

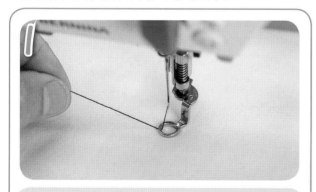

Lower the presser foot where you want to start sewing.

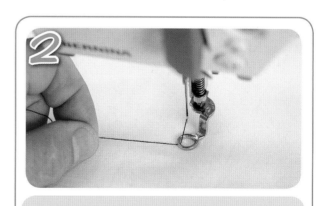

Hold the thread in your left hand.

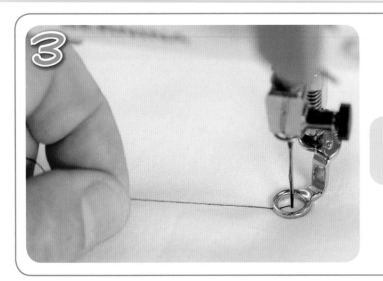

Needle down once.

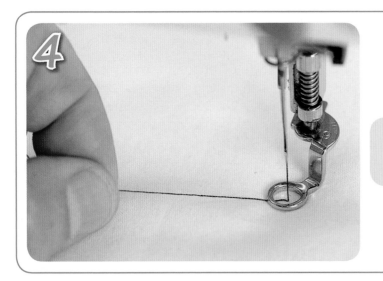

Needle up.

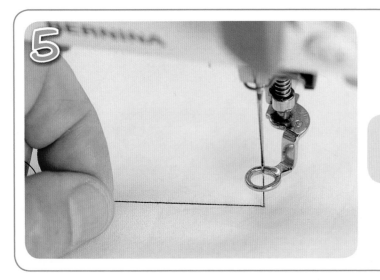

Raise the presser foot.

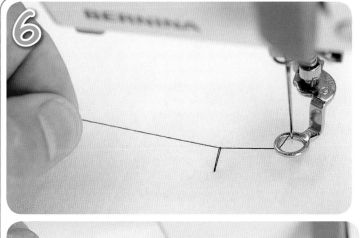

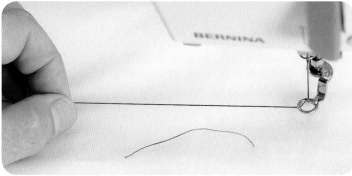

Holding the top thread in your left hand, pull the fabric toward you about 4". Tug on the top thread to pull the bobbin thread up to the top until you have a tail of thread.

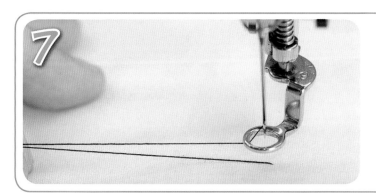

Hold the 2 threads in your left hand and return the fabric to the starting point under the needle.

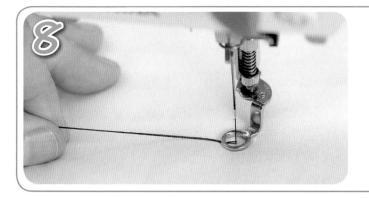

Lower the presser foot and take two stitches in place to lock the thread and start sewing.

Ending

 On your practice piece, sew about 1", then lock your thread in place (up and down 2 or 3 times in same spot).

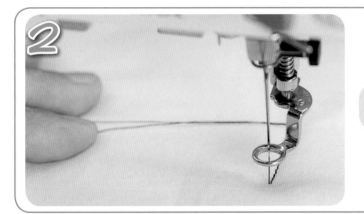

Raise the needle and the presser foot.

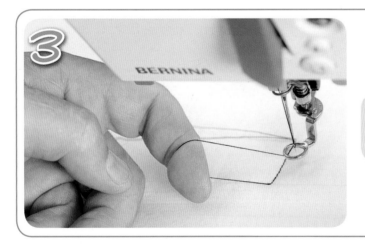

Pull the fabric toward you about 4". Loop the top thread around the finger of your left hand.

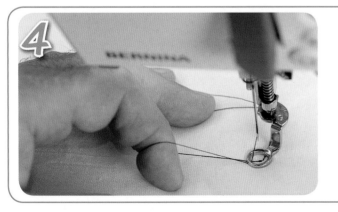

While holding the thread in a loop, place the fabric back to the ending point under the needle and lower the presser foot.

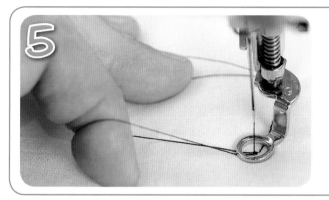

Still holding the thread, needle down, needle up once.

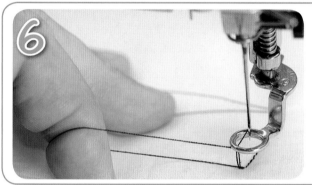

Raise the presser foot.

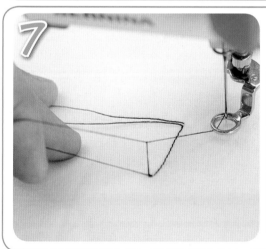
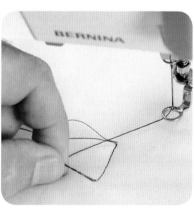

Pull the fabric toward you about 4" while pulling up on the top thread. The bobbin thread will pull through to the top of the fabric. You will have 3 threads going through the fabric to the top. The bobbin thread will not have an end, it will be a loop of two threads.

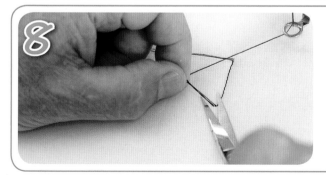

Hold all 3 threads and cut them off evenly with the fabric.

Exercise 3: Practice free-motion quilting.

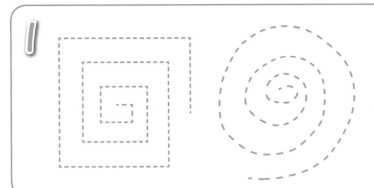

With two 12" x 12" squares of light-colored fabric, make a quilt sandwich with a piece of batting between them. Draw two "eyes" on the fabric—one squared and one rounded—with a pencil. They don't have to be perfect. They're just to provide patterns to follow.

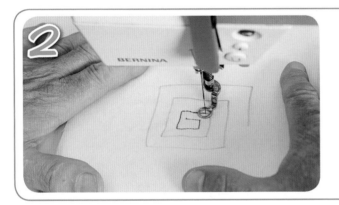

Put dark thread in your machine and bobbin. Position the needle in the center of one of the drawn patterns. Pull up the bobbin thread and start sewing, following the lines with your needle as you sew.

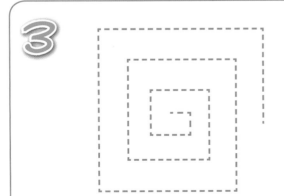

Remember—don't turn your fabric. Sew by moving the sandwich up and down, (away from and toward you) and left and right, following the straight lines.

4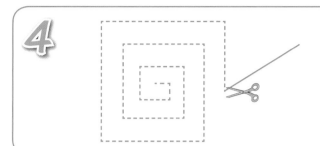

When you get to the end of the drawn design, pull the thread up and cut it.

5 Repeat on the other drawn pattern, moving the sandwich with a circular motion.

6

Check your stitches to make sure they are fairly consistent in length. Draw additional designs and practice more if you need to. Now is the time to get it right. Remember, it will not be perfect. Just get it so it looks good.

Exercise 4: Stipple on paper.

We are now going to learn how to stipple and meander. The difference between stippling and meandering is the size of the sewing pattern. A smaller pattern, with the lines of stitching about ⅛" apart, is stippling. Make larger, more open spaces, and you are meandering.

 Draw three circles that intersect, then start at the edge of one of the circles and start drawing, making direction changes and trying not to cross or come too close to another line. Keep your curves rounded, not pointed. If you want to point them later you can do anything you like, but for this practice keep them rounded.

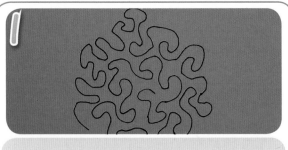

First draw a stippling design on paper.

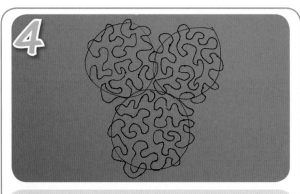

Draw outside the circle to join up with the next circle and continue drawing until the circle is filled, and so on.

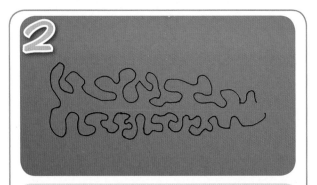

When stippling, you want your pattern to be varied consistently inconsistent, and NOT in straight lines as shown here. It should look something like a jigsaw puzzle. Never sew more than about one inch before changing directions.

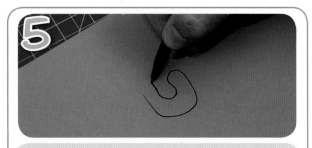

Draw a U shape and practice stitching in and out of it; change directions and stitch another U. Think of the shapes as little snake heads.

Exercise 5: Practice stippling.

Stippling is a great way to fill open space on a quilt.

Make another 12" x 12" quilt sandwich and practice stippling using the same techniques you practiced on paper.

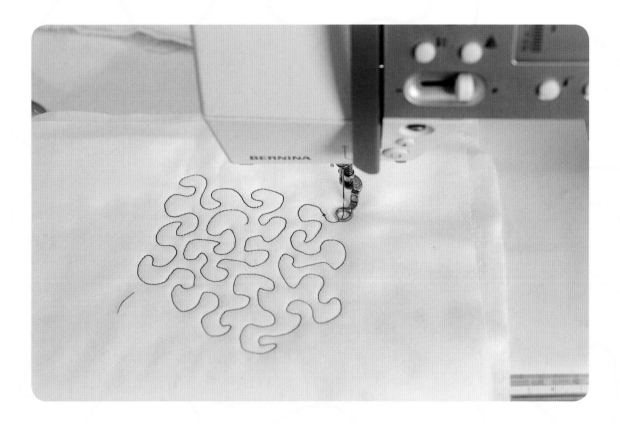

Start slowly and, if needed, draw circles on the fabric, just as you did with your earlier drawing. Then practice without drawing circles. This is one of the best practices you can do as it helps you control your stitch length and speed.

For meandering practice, trace the sample pattern on page 28.

Exercise 6: Practice feathers on paper.

Making feathers is another great way to fill space on your quilt. This exercise will show how to mark your fabric with a pattern and then sew the feather pattern.

I always use a guide to make my feathers so that I can keep them consistent in size and shape. With practice you may eventually not need the guide but if, like me, you do, it is very easy to do.

First we will practice drawing on paper.

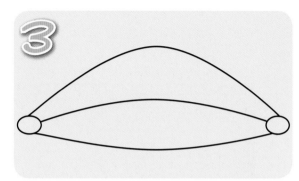

Draw a lower guideline from the bottom of one oval to the other.

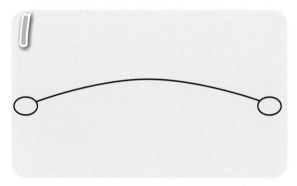

To make an outline of the feather, draw an oval, draw an arching center vein, and finish with another oval.

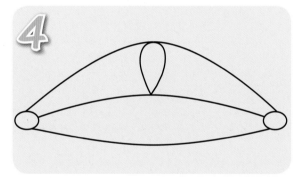

Draw a top guideline from the top of one oval to the other.

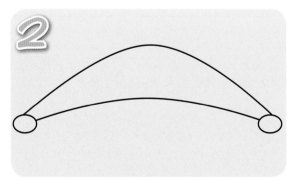

At the midpoint of the center vein, draw an upper feather.

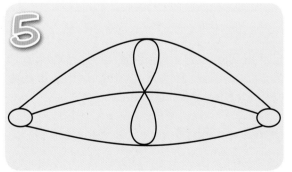

Draw a lower feather; the result is like a figure eight.

Starting at the center point of this first feather, follow up the right side of the feather, staying within the upper guideline, and draw half of a second feather, gradually returning to the starting point.

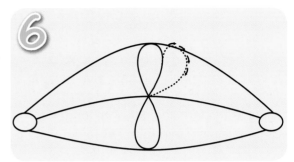

Draw a second feather.

Repeat in a similar manner for the lower half of the second feather, again returning to the starting point.

Follow the side of the second feather up. Curve this feather out and gradually draw back toward the center vein, a little way to the right of the starting point.

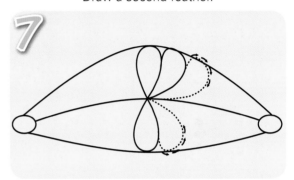

Repeat for more feathers.

Continue drawing over the vein back to the starting point. Then do the same thing on the bottom feather.

Every feather after this will not return to the center point but will gradually curve back into the center vein approximately ½" to 1" away from the last feather, depending on the shape of your feather. Continue until you have drawn all the feathers on the right side, alternating top to bottom, then return to the center point and do the same to the left side.

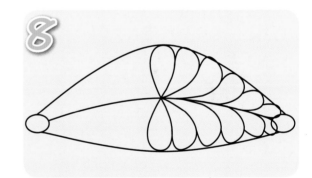

Follow up to a high point before starting to curve out.

Make sure that you follow the feather clear up toward the top before starting to draw the next feather. This will make a nice fat looking feather. Drawing out too soon will cause you to have skinny feathers.

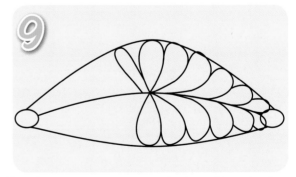

Drawing away too soon results in a skinny feather.

Exercise 7: Practice feathers on fabric.

Draw a feather design on a 12" x 12" square of fabric. Draw the two ovals and three guidelines, but only draw feathers to the right side of center. Add a second piece of fabric and batting.

Starting at the left side, sew the length of the center vein, then back to the midpoint, moving the sandwich in a gentle curve from left to right and back again. Don't turn it.

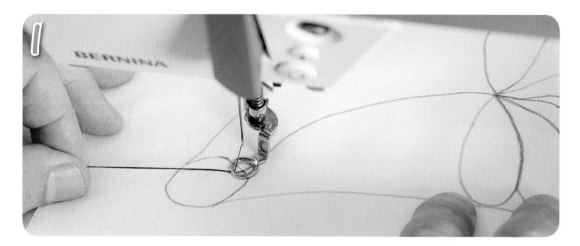

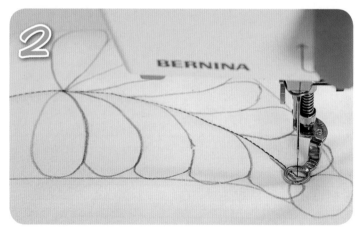

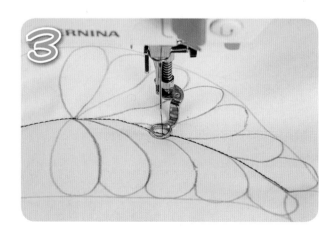

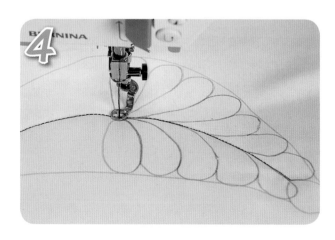

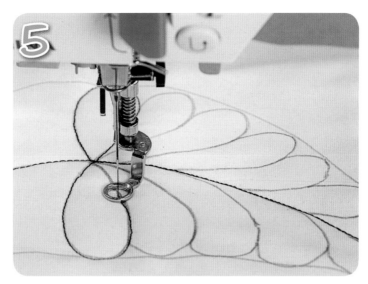

Following the drawn lines, sew the feathers, alternating from top to bottom until you get to the oval at the right end. Note that you may not have the same number of feathers on the top as you do on the bottom. This is alright.

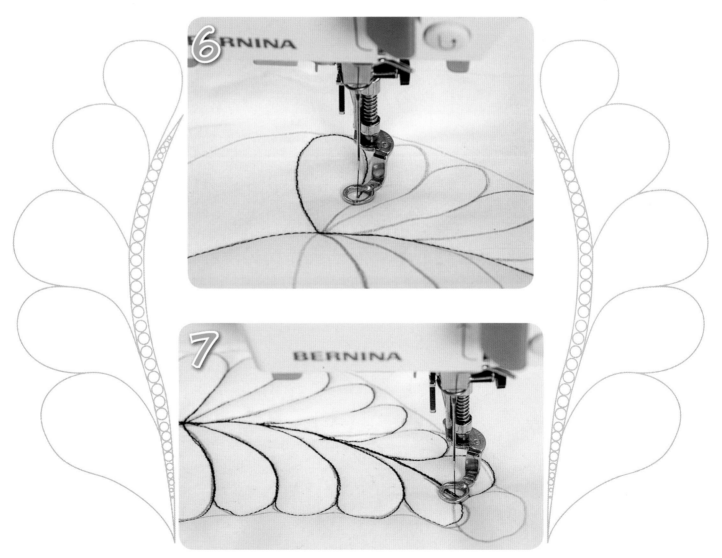

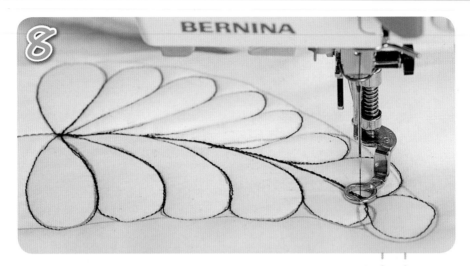

Sew around the oval to end the feather. It may or may not match the oval you drew but don't worry about that. Just sew one that fits in with the rest of the feathers.

Sew back over the center vein to the center starting point and repeat to the left side without drawing the feathers on the fabric. Sew them free motion.

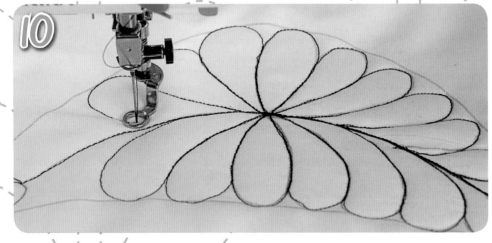

Think of it as drawing with your needle as if it is the pencil and the quilt sandwich is the paper.

Draw another feather outline. This time only draw in the center two feathers and sew as before, doing all the feathers free motion without the drawn feathers as a guide.

Do this as many times as necessary to become familiar with the process.

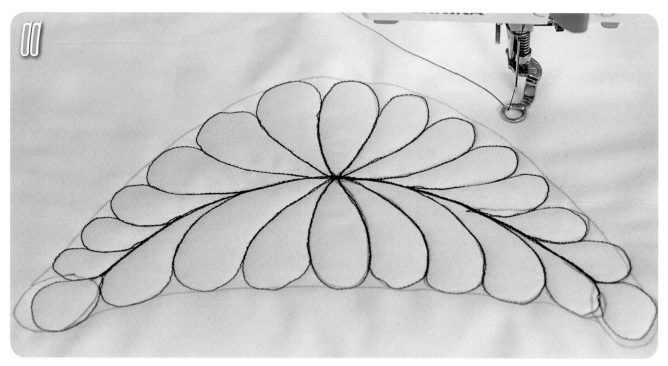

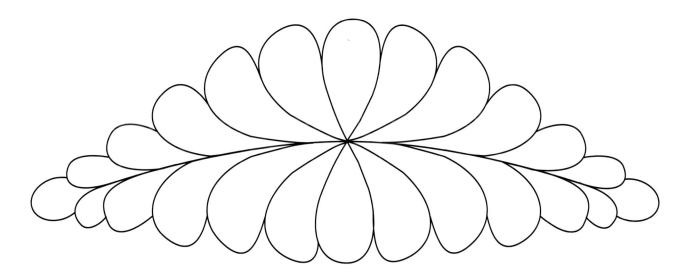

Now you are ready to do any shape or size feather that you want to fill any space you need. To fill different size spaces, draw the same size space on paper and then draw the feather to fit in the space.

Exercise 8: Practice marking your quilt.

There are several different techniques to mark patterns on your quilt. My favorite method of marking dark fabric (meaning any fabric that is not white) is by using Glad® Press'n Seal.

You can draw a picture or design, or use any picture you find that would make a good pattern. Good sources are coloring books, scroll saw books, pictures out of magazines, or designs you find on the Internet. Be careful not to infringe any copyrights. If the design is not the correct size, you can reduce or enlarge it on a copy machine.

For the practice exercise I drew a basic butterfly shape.

1 Use a piece of scrap fabric that is a little larger than your paper with the design. This fabric is used to hold the Press'n Seal.

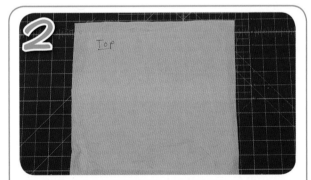

2 Place a piece of Press'n Seal (sticky side down) on the scrap fabric piece. It should be a little smaller than the fabric so it doesn't stick to anything but the fabric. Write the word TOP on it with a magic marker so you don't accidently lay it upside down and chalk the sticky side.

3 Place your drawing on top of the Press'n Seal and use a couple of pieces of painter's tape to hold it in place. (Don't use Scotch® tape as it will not come off the Press'n Seal.) The scrap fabric works only as a base to hold the Press'n Seal and picture.

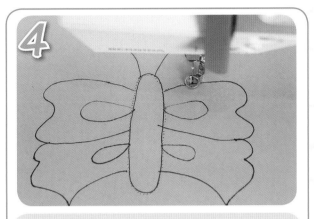

Remove the thread from your sewing machine and sew around the outline of the picture, poking holes through the paper and the Press'n Seal. Leave the detail for when you are sewing with the thread. Just make a basic outline to follow.

Tip:

You can reuse one piece of Press'n Seal several times before it will no longer stick to the quilt. If you are planning to use the pattern to make more designs on your quilt, you can make several Press'n Seal patterns at the same time by using more layers of scrap fabric with Press'n Seal on top of each piece of fabric, poking holes through all the layers at once. (For example, to make three patterns, layer fabric/Press'n Seal/fabric/Press'n Seal/fabric/Press'n Seal with the drawing on top.)

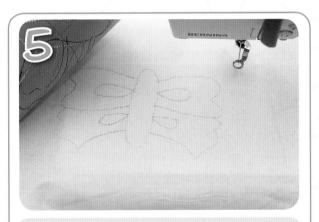

Remove the picture from the Press'n Seal.

 Carefully peel the Press'n Seal off the scrap fabric. Retain the fabric to hold the Press'n Seal when you're done.

 Use a 12" x 12" quilt sandwich with a darker fabric on top and place the Press'n Seal onto the quilt sample.

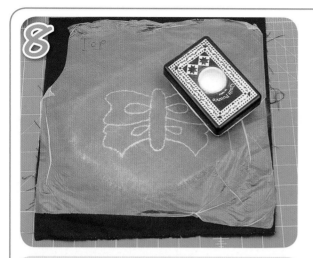

Use a white pounce pad and rub it over the holes in the Press'n Seal.

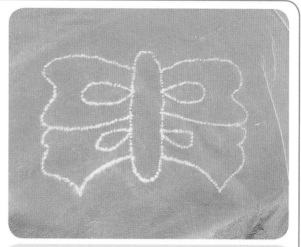

Rub it fairly hard to make sure the powder gets on the fabric well. The holes should look nice and white.

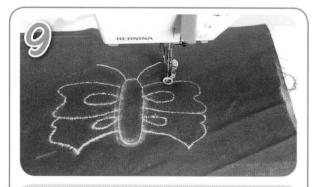

Remove the Press'n Seal and place it on the scrap fabric to hold it and keep it clean. The chalk dots will give you a very good guide to follow. The chalk will eventually rub off, so I recommend marking only three or four designs at a time.

Use the same method on white fabric using blue or red chalk. However, I urge caution as the colored chalk will not iron out and may not wash out completely. Make sure to do a test sample on a small piece of the fabric you will be using and wash it to make sure it will come out. I have had some fabric where you can still see the blue chalk even after washing.

Marking White Fabric

Using a Light Box

This is a method I use to mark designs on white fabric on a quilt top before I have assembled the quilt sandwich.

Draw the design onto plain white paper with an ink pen or dark lead pencil or use a copy.

Tape the paper onto a light box.

Place the quilt top over the pattern on the light box, aligning the quilting location on the quilt with the pattern. The pattern will show through the fabric.

Using a water-soluble pen, trace the pattern onto the quilt top.

Mark the entire quilt top as lightly as possible while still being able to see the markings. Then make a sandwich with the marked fabric, batting, and backing. Quilt following the drawn design.

If you don't have a light box you can purchase a piece of Plexiglas® from a hardware store and position a light under it.

Using a Template

Another method of marking white fabric is to draw your design onto a thin plastic sheet (most quilt shops carry this) or a piece of thicker paper and cut out the design. Place this template onto the quilt and mark around the template using a water-soluble pen. Mark as lightly as possible.

This works well on quilts where you have already assembled the quilt sandwich.

The marks can be removed by washing the quilt or spritzing the quilt with water from a spray bottle. If you spritz the marks, be advised that some of the marks will return when the water dries. If the marks do return, go ahead and spritz again. You may have to do this a few times to get all the marks removed.

Using Press'n Seal

Another method is to draw the design right onto Press'n Seal, then place it onto the quilt and sew over the Press'n Seal following the pattern. Then peel the Press'n Seal off the quilt. Use a blunt end tool to help peel up the Press'n Seal in corner areas.

Quilting by Zones

I use a "quilting by zones" method. The purpose is to isolate sections of the quilt and hold the fabrics and batting in place. There are two methods of quilting by zones.

If there are readily available zones (for example, the quilt top is made of blocks), you can stitch in the ditch between the zones. Otherwise, you can create zones using water-soluble thread.

Stitch in the Ditch

If the quilt is made of squares or rectangles, stitch in the ditch around every block starting in the middle and working toward the outside of the quilt.

Another option is to sew down and across each major seam, which will have the same effect as stitching around each square.

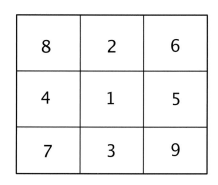

Sew around each square in this order.

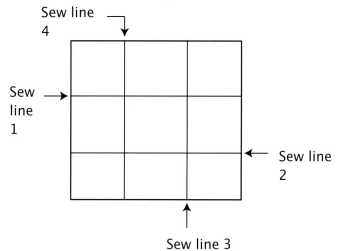

Then consider each area or zone as a separate quilt. Do your detailed quilting in each zone without worrying about the fabric moving in any of the other zones.

Water-Soluble Thread

Sew grids on the quilt with water-soluble thread in both the needle and bobbin. Quilt as you normally would, ignoring the water-soluble thread creating the zones. When you are finished quilting, spritz the water-soluble grid with water to dissolve it or dissolve it by washing the quilt.

This method eliminates the possibility of the fabric puckering on the top or bottom.

It is best to start quilting in the middle zones and work your way out toward the sides. If you start on the outside zones first, the quilting will make the quilt stiffer and it will be more difficult to stuff it through the machine.

Handling Bulk

When working on a large quilt, do not roll it up. Stuff the quilt into the machine. This allows you room to slide your hand under the bulk of the quilt where it is stuffed to the right of the needle in the throat of the machine, giving you more control moving the quilt under the needle.

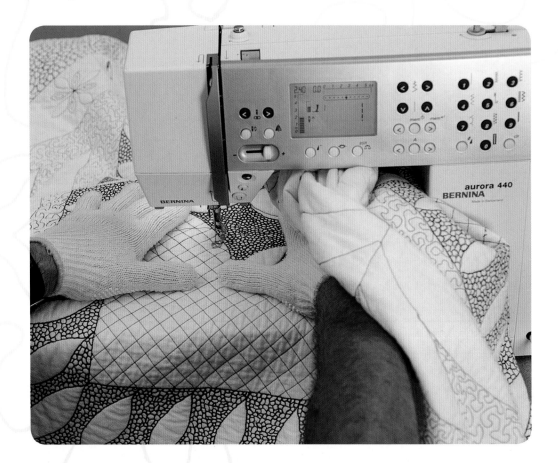

"Quilt As Desired"

Finally, let's discuss those three dreaded little words that often appear at the end of quilt instructions: QUILT AS DESIRED. If you are like me, I don't usually have a clue as to how I am going to quilt my quilts after they are pieced.

The first thing I do is lay the quilt on the floor and stare at it. Sometimes, I will leave it there until the next day and look at it again. I will look at the fabrics in the quilt and see if there is any design that appeals to me. If so, I will incorporate that in my quilting design.

For example, if there are flowers in any of the fabrics, I may use a similar flower design for some of my quilting. I will see what open spaces there are in the quilt and decide what might look good to fill in the spaces, such as stippling or feathers.

My best advice: use your imagination.

More AQS Books

This is only a small selection of the books available from the American Quilter's Society. AQS books are known worldwide for timely topics, clear writing, beautiful color photos, and accurate illustrations and patterns. The following books are available from your local bookseller, quilt shop, or public library.

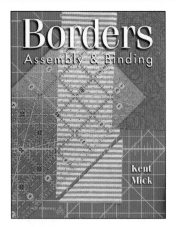

#1586 .... $12.95

#1590 .... $12.95

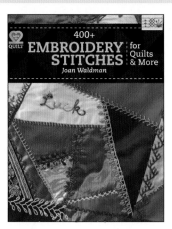

#1274 .... $12.95

#1278 .... $12.95

#1275 .... $12.95

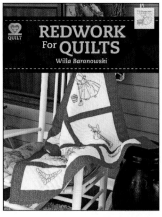

#1273 .... $12.95

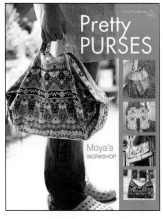

#1589 .... $12.95

#1280 .... $12.95

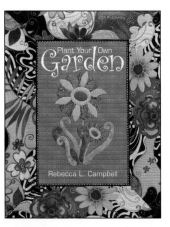

#1583 .... $12.95

LOOK for these books nationally.
CALL or VISIT our website at

1-800-626-5420
www.AmericanQuilter.com